ETERNALLY MAD

Edited by
Albert B. Feldstein

WARNER BOOKS

A Warner Communications Company

OOPED

ARTIST: ANGELO TORRES

WRITER: ARNIE KOGEN

You **don't understand, Man!** I've got the **HEADS!** They all use me . . . the **grooviest broads in Beverly Hills** . . . Sally Fields, Barbara Rush, Jill St. John, Eydie Gorme, Angie Dickinson, Hermione Gingold, Maria Ouspenskaya, Gale Storm, Wayne Newton, Tony Orlando and Dawn and Dino and Desi and Liberace!

Those references are a **farce,** Mr. Carlyle! This is a **respected Beverly Hills Bank,** dealing in **conservative financial investments** typical of all Southern California Banking Institutions!

Yes— and don't ever **come back** to the **Joan Blondell Bank and Trust Co.!**

You **creep!** You mean you're **turning me down?**

Kawasaki lets the good times roll ♪. .
Kawasaki lets the good times roll ♪. .

Hi, Baby! What's new?

Why didn't you **call** me, **Gorgeous**? Why do you leave me **all alone** in this **canyon house**? Why weren't you **here** with me?

That's **just** what I need in my **life** right now . . . **another** sensational—looking, sick, sex-starved, neurotic woman!

I been thinking about my **career**, Jilt! I'm kinda **fed up** down at the Beauty Shop! I want to open my **own place**!

I understand how you **feel**! You're trying to **FIND yourself**! You're not really **happy** with your life!

Yeah! On the **other** hand, I really **can't COMPLAIN** about my life! After all . . . there are Make-Out Men in **INDIA** that are **STARVING**!!

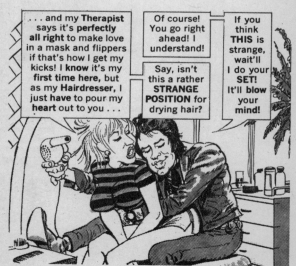

Well, here we are at "The Bistro!" Now . . . let's get our **roles** straight! **Jerkie**, I'm escorting **you**, who has the hots for me but is being "**kept**" by **Lesser**, whose **Wife** and **Daughter** I've just had an "**affair**" with! **Jilt**, here, is my **Girlfriend**, who thinks I'm **faithful**, but in her **frustration**, is getting **even** with me by dating **Jaunty** who's trying to put the **make** on her and take her to **Egypt!** Jaunty . . . you're **new** in this crowd! What do you **think** of it?

This is certainly the most **immoral** group of individuals our **Society** has **ever** produced!

Hey, **quiet**, everyone! **Nixon** and **Agnew** are going to speak!

Wait! I take it **back!** The **SECOND** most immoral group!

Oh, **Felandera**, **there** you are! I'd like you to **meet** everyone! You **know** Gorgeous! And this is **Jilt**, and **Jaunty** . . . and this is **Jerkie**! Er . . . say, it's awfully **quiet** in here, with everyone staring **daggers** at each other! We could sure **use** something to **break** the **tension** . . .

ONE DAY ON THE HIGHWAY

THE LIGHTER SIDE OF... INDOOR

GARD

Consider the **history of Mankind!** In the beginning, the **jungle** was **dangerous** and **threatening!** And so, for **comfort** and **safety,** Man moved inside **protective dwellings!**

Today, Civilization has reached **great heights!** And yet, Mankind **still** feels threatened and in danger! So we've **reversed** the process! **Today,** for comfort . . .

AND OUTDOOR

eNING

ARTIST & WRITER: DAVE BERG

...we bring the **JUNGLE** inside our **dwellings**, as my **Wife** has done!

You said it, Pal!

Including the **WATERFALLS!**

You see that? The economic situation sure is bad!

It's not that bad!

Just look around you! People are growing their own vegetables! That shows you things aren't going so well!

It all depends on your point of view!

In the Great Depression, people planted vegetable gardens in empty lots . . . just like they're doing today! That proves things are desperate!

Well, as I see it, things are booming!

I'm in the SEED BUSINESS!!

What a healthy-looking vegetable garden!

Well, it gave me plenty of trouble! I really wanted a successful garden this year, but I ran into a problem!

Weeds kept sprouting and choking off the seedling plants! I started a real battle with them, raking —and pulling them out— and using weed killers!

Well, you must've won the battle! You have a beautiful crop . . .!

Actually, I lost the battle!

Those are the WEEDS!!

Hey, you gotta see Noah Seaman's **garden**! It's only as big as a **postage stamp**, but he **works** it like it's a big-time **farm** operation!

Hey, Noah! How's your **tomato crop** coming along?

Not growing **tomatoes**! This year, it's **carrots**!

What's the **matter**? Did you get **tired** of **eating all** those **tomatoes**?

You know how it is with **us** farmers!

I'm ROTATING MY CROPS!

I see you have **quite a collection of plants!** There are so many **varieties** of plants, and all of them have **names** . . . like *Guzmania Lingulata* and *Tillandsia Ionantha!* Do **you** know the **names** of YOUR plants . . . ?

I sure do . . . most intimately!

This one is **"Irving,"** and this one is **"Gloria,"** and this one is **"Sidney,"** and this one is **"Carol,"** and—

How do you keep your **lawn** looking so **lush**?

I **water** it **religiously** . . . every single day!

But . . . what if you're not home?

I've got an **automatic timer** that turns the **sprinkler** on at the same time every day!

Speaking of time, what time is it **NOW**?

I **don't** have a **watch** with me!

But I can **tell** you . . . it's precisely seven o'clock!!

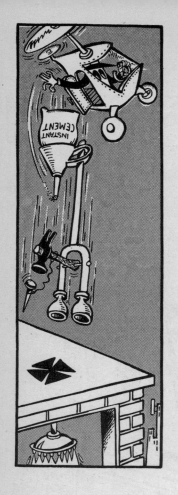
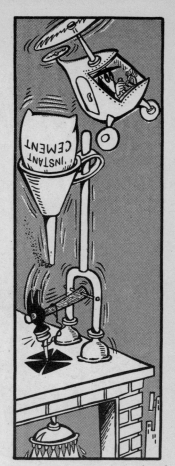

History has recorded the famous words uttered by famous men . . . words that we all know well. But did it ever occur to you that maybe the other people present didn't just stand around applauding when those words were said . . . that maybe somebody else had an answer or a topper or some equally important words to say in rebuttal . . . only we're not familiar with those words because they're the

ZAPPERS THAT HISTORY FORGOT

ARTIST: GEORGE WOODBRIDGE

WRITER: ALEN ROBIN

Who Knows What Evils Lurk In The Hearts Of Men?

THE SHADOW KNOWS

WRITER & ARTIST: SERGIO ARAGONES

Tonight . . . live . . . from the fabulous **Men's Public Toilet**, located in the sensational basement of the spectacular **Kennedy Center For The Performing Arts**, here in beautiful downtown **Washington, D.C.**, we bring you **The First Annual Presentation Ceremonies of . . .**

MAD'S ACADEMY AWARDS FOR PUBLIC SERVANTS

Yes, folks . . . all of the "greats" and "near-greats" in Public Service have gathered here tonight to honor their fellow professionals who have given performances throughout the year that are unmatched in Private Industry . . .

. . . those so-called "little people" who actually make our country work . . . sometimes, not so well . . . and sometimes even worse! Yes, folks, they are the people who may not be very good in their assigned jobs—

—but who, by their great ACTING ABILITY, manage to escape having their uselessness detected until they retire from office at public expense! And now . . . on with the show! The envelopes, please . . .

The Runner-Up in The "Internal Revenue Service" Category is Mr. Alan Wince for his performance before a Senate Hearing in "We're Only Human!"

WRITER: STAN HART   ARTIST: GEORGE WOODBRIDGE

Mr. Wince, as head of the I.R.S., please explain how your Department could overlook Mr. Nixon's failure to pay nearly $500,000 in taxes, and Mr. Rockefeller's failure to pay over $600,000 in taxes!
I'm glad you asked that, Senator! You see, my Department is extremely understaffed! My people are working four, maybe five days a week, three maybe four hours a day! It's just not humanly possible to check out everyone's tax return!

You mean that many tax returns go unchecked!?
Not many! We check out returns of everyone making under $15,000 a year! Those little guys can really cheat!
Isn't it true that you forgot to check Mr. Nixon's return because he appointed you to your job?!?
Gosh . . . I can't remember WHO appointed me! But I'll be glad to look it up, right after I check out YOUR return, Sir!
Er . . . maybe you'd better forget the whole thing!

... and the Winner in The "Internal Revenue Service" Category is Mr. Melvin Slasher for his outstanding rendition of "I Am Your Friend!"

Now, don't you be nervous about this Tax Audit! Your Government wants you to claim every deduction, and we of the I.R.S. are here to help you!

Okay ... let's see! Entertainment Expenses ... Disallowed! Medical Expenses ... Disallowed! Charity Contributions ... Disallowed! You owe the Government—hmm—$1000!!

I DID! Your Government's now $1000 richer! And what's good for the U.S. of A. is good for you!

$1000?!? But ... I thought you said you were going to help me!

A brilliant performance! It's just too bad that the poor guy had to pay that $1000!

He could've saved $500 by implementing The Auditor's Forgiveness Clause!

How does that work?

Simple! He merely deposits $500 in my personal Swiss Bank Account, and I forgive and forget!

In The "Police" Category, the Runner-Up is Officer Victor Manure for his compelling "It's Up To You!"

How do you do, Ma'am? Your local Police Force is trying to raise money for its Retirement Fund, and we're going around, selling these raffles!

Oh, I'm afraid I'm a little short of cash . . . !

That's perfectly all right! We don't want you to feel pressured in any way! It's just that you get one of these "Friends Of The Force" car decals with every book of raffles that you buy . . .

But I don't put decals on my car!

Well, Ma'am, you'd better have THIS one on if you're ever stopped by a Cop in this town!

Oh? Yes!! I'll take TWO . . . one for each car!

How about the kids' bikes?! You never know when one of 'em will go through a "Stop" sign!!

... and the Winner in The "Police" Category is Officer Roy "Guts" Gentry for his competent and detailed crime report in "Telling It Like It Is"

Officer Gentry, can you tell our viewing audience just what happened?

Certainly! I attempted to apprehend the alleged suspect when the suspect attracted my attention while I was performing my function as the legal presiding peace officer of the prescribed area!

As I approached, the suspect immediately gave me adequate rationale to remove my service revolver from its holster and discharge several missiles in order to forestall additional and untoward danger to the tranquility of the community!

Congratulations for that **competent** and **detailed** delivery, Officer Gentry . . . but—er—could you tell us what happened in a little **shorter** version!

Sure! I plugged the ⊛✦⊙⍟☂✷✱# for **talking back** to me when I tried to stop him for **Jay-Walking**!

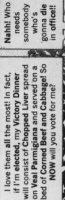

. . . and the **Winner** is Congressman-elect **Charles A. Bleadinhardt** for his conscience-provoking, heart-rending **"We're All In This Together!"**
I'm **saddened** by the sight of **unemployed men** and **women** hanging around **street corners!**
I'm **heartbroken** when I see the **filth** and the **decay** that is destroying our **great cities!**
I am **terrorized** and **frightened** by the **violence** and **crime** that runs rampant in our streets!
I **don't want to see** these things **any longer!** They make me **SICK!** That's why you **must** send me to **Washington!!**
SALE
DRIED PRUNES
Congratulations on your **inspiring performance!** But tell us, what are you going to do to **eliminate** all these problems?
Not a **thing!**
But you said that **seeing** those things makes you **sick . . . !**
Right! That's why I wanted to be sent to **Washington . . .** where I **won't** have to see them! *Heh-heh!*

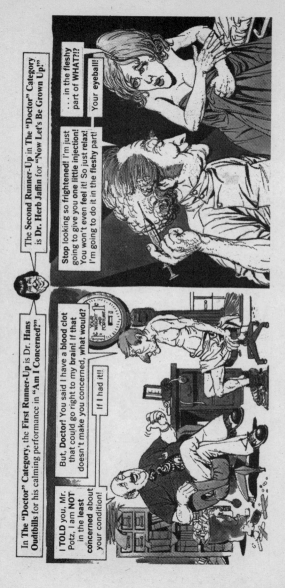

The **Winner** in **The "Nurse" Category** is R.N. **Elsa Kotch** for her tender, sensitive, emphatic rendition of **"Listen, I've Only Got Two Hands!"**
Demands, demands, **demands!** That's all I **hear** all day long! "Get me **this!**"... "Get me **that!**" What do you think I **am**—a **machine?!?** Lord, can't a person have a **single minute's rest?!?**
But **I haven't rung before!** I've been in a **COMA** for the past two weeks!
Stop making **excuses** and try to think of **someone else** besides **yourself** for once in your life! Now, you just **lie there quietly** till I can find the time to come back!
Congratulations! You certainly **deserve** this! Tell us, did that little old lady **learn** anything from your talk?
Oh, yes! She became **very cooperative!**
Really? What did she **do?**
She went back into her **coma** for **another** two weeks!

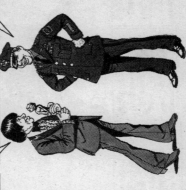

Second Runner-Up is recently appointed Ambassador **Ruth Mestermission** for her **"Friend From Overseas!"**

As the representative of my great nation, I want to say how happy I am to be here in your great nation! And I want to guarantee to you all that our great nation will never interfere with the legitimate aims and goals of your great nation!

In America, we respect different political and ideological views! And so, even though your form of Government is not OUR form of Government, we still admire your people!

Ya zah gret mah bucci la!

And God bless you, my child!

That's terrible! The child said, "Yankee ass, go home!!" Won't that offend the new Ambassador?

How could it? No American Ambassador has ever bothered to learn ours... or any OTHER foreign language!

...and the **Winner** is the Government of the U.S. for its performance in "Our Red Brothers!" Accepting will be Mr. Wilson Heap of "The Bureau Of Indian Affairs"...

We of the Government are committed to seeing that the Indian gets all that's coming to him! We dedicate ourselves to preserving the age-old traditions that are so important to the Red Man!

Very touching indeed! It's nice to know that the U.S. Government is dedicated to preserving the Indian's age-old traditions of tribal identity, freedom and access to open spaces!

Nahh! I meant the WHITE MAN'S age-old traditions of keeping the Indian poverty-stricken, powerless and without any hope!

Well, that wraps up **MAD's Academy Awards For Public Servants!** And if it proves nothing else, it shows that we certainly have a **National Theater** like in **England!** The only difference is: **Here**, we call our Theater **"Civil Service"** and our actors **"Public Servants"!** Bye ...

LATE ONE AFTERNOON IN A DOCTOR'S OFFICE

IN AN EFFORT TO FIGHT INFLATION,
BY SCREWING THE OIL CARTELS
AND THE UTILITY COMPANIES,
YOUR IDIOT EDITORS NOW PRESENT...

SOME MAD ENERGY-SAVING DEVICES

ARTIST: BOB CLARKE   WRITER: PAUL PETER PORGES

THE WINDMILL-POWERED PENCIL SHARPENER

THE PENDULUM-PROPELLED CARVING KNIFE

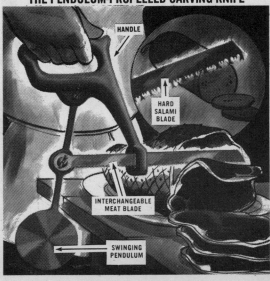

HANDLE

HARD SALAMI BLADE

INTERCHANGEABLE MEAT BLADE

SWINGING PENDULUM

THE POGO-STICK-ACTIVATED HIGH-SPEED BLENDER

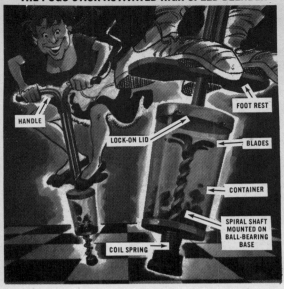

HANDLE

LOCK-ON LID

FOOT REST

BLADES

CONTAINER

SPIRAL SHAFT MOUNTED ON BALL-BEARING BASE

COIL SPRING

THE COMBINATION STOOL & WATER PICK

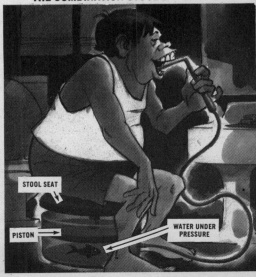

STOOL SEAT

PISTON

WATER UNDER PRESSURE

THE SELF-GENERATING ELECTRIC GUITAR

THE PUSH-PEDAL-POWERED VACUUM CLEANER

THE WIND-UP RUBBER-BAND-DRIVEN POWER TOOL

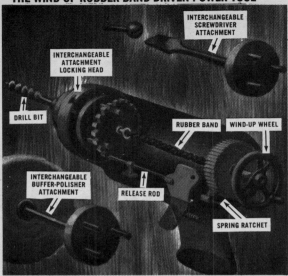

INTERCHANGEABLE
SCREWDRIVER
ATTACHMENT

INTERCHANGEABLE
ATTACHMENT
LOCKING HEAD

DRILL BIT

RUBBER BAND   WIND-UP WHEEL

INTERCHANGEABLE
BUFFER-POLISHER
ATTACHMENT

RELEASE ROD

SPRING RATCHET

THE SOLAR-ENERGIZED CORDLESS HOT COMB

A MAD LOOK AT

WRINKS

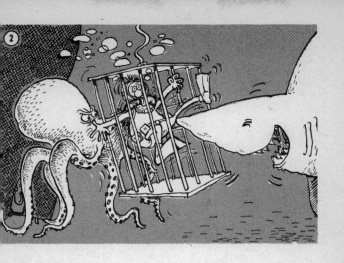

WH AT'S

WO RSE

THAN...?

ARTIST: JACK RICKARD   WRITER: ALIS ELLIS

WHAT'S WORSE THAN...

...a teacher droning on
and on for a whole period?

MID-TERM
EXAM
TODAY

A teacher not saying a
word for a whole period!

WHAT'S WORSE THAN...

...having to work on a Holiday?

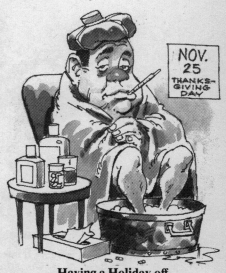

Having a Holiday off and being sick!

WHAT'S WORSE THAN...

...losing a contact lens?

Finding it unexpectedly!

WHAT'S WORSE THAN...

... listening to the kids
bang around and make noise?

Nothing but silence ... and
you know they're up there!

WHAT'S WORSE THAN...

... no letter from home?

A letter from home with no check!

WHAT'S WORSE THAN...

... being sent down to the Principal's office alone?

Being in the Principal's office with your Parents!

WHAT'S WORSE THAN...

...making a
costly mistake?

**Having someone else find it
before you can correct it!**

WHAT'S WORSE THAN...

... bringing lunch to school?

Buying it in the cafeteria!

Hello, out there! Welcome to **Dry Talk Country!** (That's a little local New York joke!) I'm **George Slimton!** As you all know, I've done some really dangerous and foolhardy things in my time . . . like scrimmaging against a **pro football team,** and stepping into a ring with a **boxing champion,** and photographing a **charging elephant!** But they were all child's play compared to this assignment: Conducting one of those idiotic interviews for **MAD Magazine!** Not that it's **more dangerous** . . . just **more embarrassing** than those other embarrassing things I've done! Anyway, today we're going to meet Lester Loudmouth, who has been selected as . . .

MAD'S OBNOXIOUS SPORTS SPECTATOR OF THE YEAR

ARTIST: JACK DAVIS   WRITER: LOU SILVERSTONE

C'mon! We'll be late!

But the game doesn't start for an hour!

I wanna get there for the warmup!

What was your biggest thrill in sports?

I've had lots of thrills! Like last year, when Jerry West made a basket just as the buzzer went off . . . !

Did it win the game?

Nah! They lost by **9 points**! But the basket beat the point spread, and I won a few bucks!

Er—is bothering people the **ONLY** reason you enjoy attending sporting events, Lester?

Course not!

Then you **DO** enjoy the thrill of competition?!?

Not exactly! I like to see guys get hurt!

It's Giants ball, first and ten!

Another thing I like to do is listen to a DIFFERENT game on my portable radio! It drives everybody around me up the wall!

Hey! Turn that %$#& thing off!!

Where are you going?
It's time for the kickoff!

Me? I'm goin' for a hot dog! I ALWAYS go during kickoffs and other crucial plays! It really bugs people! Hey, Mac, would you mind gettin' out of my way? Cheez! Some people ain't got no manners at all!

You are a fan— wanting to see the players warm up!

What players?!? I wanna warm up!

NAMATH, YOU'RE A %$#@& STIFF!

CASTER, YOU GOT CEMENT HANDS!

WINNERS?!? YOU'RE ALL LOSERS!

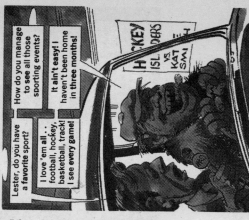

Lester, do you have a favorite sport?

I love 'em all... football, hockey, basketball, track! I see every game!

How do you manage to see all those sporting events?

It ain't easy! I haven't been home in three months!

HOCKEY
ISL ...DERS
VS.
KAT SMI ...H

C'mon! Let's go!

It is as far as I'm concerned! My flask of booze is empty—and I'll freeze!

But the game's not over yet!

In SEPTEMBER...?!?

I'll tell you one thing! I know this game! I would've made a really great Coach!

C'MON! PASS THE BALL! PUT IT IN THE AIR!

The other team intercepted!

Namath, you dumb bum!! Why didn't you stay on the ground?!?

Yeah! There's not much action, but I get my kicks! Listen—

See that? The dummy thought the Linesman made that "Out" call, and he let the ball go! Now he'll start an argument ... and the fans'll boo him for unsportsman-like conduct!

Watch ... OUT!!

BOOO!

BOOO!

Off the court!!

What about boxing? You didn't mention it! Do you like boxing?

I used to go, but the real fight fans are gone! Now, all you see are cats in far-out costumes attending the big bouts! They don't care about the sport! They just go so people'll stare at 'em! Once in a while, I'll go when two Spanish guys are fighting! No matter who wins, there's always a riot ... with throwing chairs and fun like that! But boxing is DEAD as a spectator sport! Gi'me a good TRACK MEET ... any time!

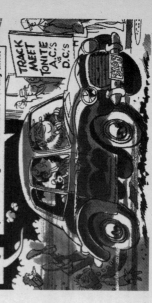

Lester, you attend many baseball games! What do you think is wrong with baseball today? Not enough super stars? Or is the action too slow?

The main thing wrong with baseball today is that the Sody Pop and Beer is sold in paper cups! How can you conk somebody with a paper cup?!? In the old days, drinks were sold in BOTTLES! THAT was exciting baseball!!

BASEBALL
CAT FISH vs
ORIOLES

YOU'RE A BUM, WILT! MY TEN-YEAR-OLD KID SHOOTS BETTER THAN YOU!!!

Ah, button your lip, you creep!

Did you hear that? Man, I don't know what sports are comin' to! A fan can't even open his mouth! I'm payin' that stiff's salary! Didn't he ever hear of the 5th Amendment, Freedom of Speech?!?!

Whatever! It means a person's allowed to express an opinion! It's a free country!

That's the Bill of Rights . . .!

Another game that stands out in my memory is the day the Mets won the Pennant! We tore up the turf and the bases, and wrecked the stadium! Boy, that was some day!

I guess you took everything that wasn't nailed down, eh?

Man, we took it, whether it was nailed down or not!

What was your most exciting moment as a baseball spectator?

There's one game I'll never forget!

Was it during a World Series?

No, it was on "Beer Day"! Beer was selling for five cents a cup! Man, the joint was really jumpin'! It got so wild, the game was called—and the Home Team hadda forfeit it!

DON MARTIN

THE

BEATS
HIGH COST
OF GASOLINE

KLIK VROOM SPOOSH

THE LIGHTER SIDE OF...

MAKING EXTRA MONEY

ARTIST & WRITER: DAVE BERG

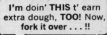

And this is my **Son** . . . the **clever entrepreneur!** He collects **old comic books** and **carefully preserves** them in **protective plastic bags!** Go ahead, Son . . . **tell** Emily what they're **worth!**

Well, these comic books are **Collectors' Items!** I can sell them for **big money** at Comic Book Conventions! F'rinstance, I could get **$300** for this old "**Superman**" comic . . . and **$250** for this old "**Batman**" comic . . .

. . . and **$500** for this "**Shock SuspenStories Number Three**" . . . and **$1000** for this "**Panic**" . . .

Wow! You certainly are an **enterprising young man!** You're going to be worth a **small fortune** when you sell them!

SELL them?!? Are you out of your **mind**?!? I wouldn't give up a **single one** of these books for the **world!**

Sir, I'll shovel the **snow** off your side walk for a **reasonable price**!

Son! You've got a **deal**!

I **can't believe it!** When I was a kid **we** made extra money by doing back-breaking work, but I thought kids of today were so **spoiled** and **soft**, they wouldn't ever **take on** manual labor jobs! Yet, **here's** a kid willing to work up a **sweat**!

You're **right!** He's working up a **sweat** all right . . .

That's a pretty long walk from our **front door** to his Father's **gas powered snow-blower!!**

Look, George! Stop the car! Somebody's having a **Garage Sale** . . . and you **know** how I simply **adore** Garage Sales!

People are suckers! They can't resist what they think are **bargains** . . . and they buy up all the **junk** other people are trying to get **rid** of!

That's **right**, George!

And **you're** the **worst sucker** of **all!** You've spent a **fortune** on these stupid Garage Sales!

That's **right**, George!

Except that **I'll** make it all **back** with a **profit**, when I hold a **Garage Sale** of my own!

TAKE IT WITH A GRAIN OF SALT WHEN...

ARTIST: JACK DAVIS   WRITER: LOU SILVERSTONE

...the head of a Teachers Union says they're striking for higher wages so the kids will get a better education.

...a businessman says yes, he gave a politician a half million bucks, but he never expected anything in return.

. . . the President pardons the man who appointed him to the job, and then claims that there was no deal.

. . . the owner of a team that has dropped ten straight games gives his Coach a vote of confidence.

. . . a Union Leader, whose members get $15.00 an hour, blames the Government for inflation and rising unemployment.

. . . the Coach of a basketball factory who has just lost his star player to a million dollar Pro contract says he feels the kid is making a mistake by not completing his education.

. . . the Mayor of a large city takes a brief walk accompanied by half the Police Force and dozens of reporters, and says, "The city is perfectly safe!"

. . . a veteran quarterback who's pulling down $125,000 a year says he's unhappy because he hasn't seen enough action.

. . . a lumber company's ads proclaim they are doing great things for our forests.

. . . the commercials for a mediocre movie saturate your TV screen, claiming that millions of people saw and loved the film no matter what the critics said about it.

. . . a former Government Official, famous for paying attention to the smallest detail, when questioned about a huge graft payoff, says, "I can't recall!"

. . . anybody assures you that "the check is in the mail."

...a TV Network proudly announces that this will be their finest season ever.

...a badly beaten fighter claims he got a fast count from the Referee.

. . . the President assures us that we can beat inflation by wearing a "win" button.

. . . a magazine charges 50¢—
and then claims it's "cheap."

BEAT THE RECESSION WITH THESE HELPFUL

MAD PENNY-PINCHING HINTS

ARTIST: PAUL COKER, JR.
WRITER: PAUL PETER PORGES

Buy your perishables before week-end
closing time . . . when you can bargain.

Eliminate unnecessary Doctor bills. Brush up on "Home Remedies"
and take care of your family's minor medical problems by yourself.

Encourage your kids to build appropriate Birthday, Wedding or Bar Mitzvah gifts in your home (or their school) workshop.

CORKS FLOAT — keep half of
teaBag dry — for Later use.

Tea

PIN

CORKS

Invent clever money-saving methods like this "Teabag-Saver" which keeps half the teabag dry for later use.

Have your kids design and execute . . . and then hand deliver . . . your family's Christmas Cards.

Have your kids bring home their Free School Lunch leftovers in Doggie Bags.

Give your family homemade haircuts.

Spray on socks with washable paint.

Grow or produce your own Gourmet food.

For entertainment, return to the simple (and cheap) ways of yore.

Give your kids interest-bearing notes instead of their usual cash allowance.

Save fuel by saving hot water. Bathe "Japanese Family Style."

Drop in on your rich relatives during their mealtimes.

Use any available free transportation.

Keep your food budget low. Tell disgusting stories at the table.

Start wearing old, patched clothes
. . . and pretend you're "with it."

Scan local newspapers and clip those
special "Sale" and "Money-off" coupons.

Eliminate expensive reading material! Send
for interesting free Government pamphlets.

Get together with your neighbors and friends and form "Magazine Pools."

When in need of professional advice,
try consulting experts casually at parties.

If necessary, use alternate means
of long-distance communications.

Make your own toilet paper.

ONE
FINE DAY
DURING
LUNCH
PERIOD

DUM-DUM AFTERNOON

For a while there, we were being treated to a rash of bank robbery films in which the criminals were clever, their plans ingenious and the execution brilliant. However, we are now threatened with a new, sickening trend in bank robbery films . . . inspired by the success of this latest farce . . . in which the criminals are IDIOTS who get themselves all loused up one hot

ARTIST: MORT DRUCKER

WRITER: LARRY SIEGEL

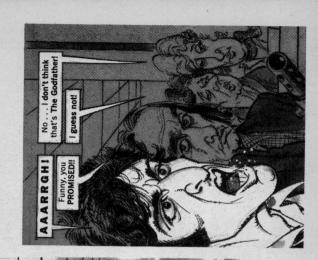

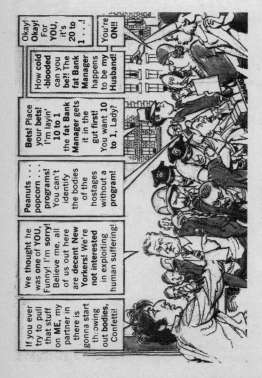

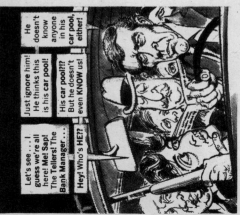